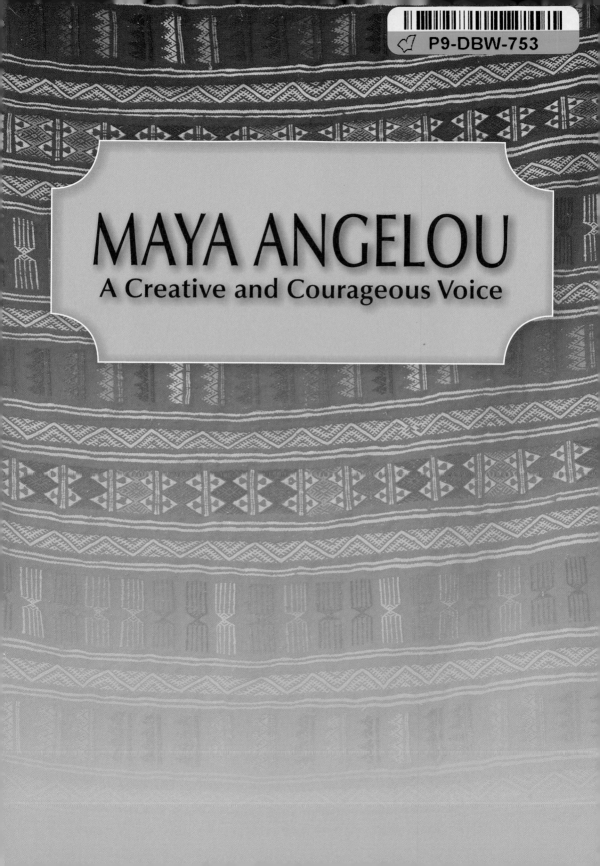

MAYA ANGELOU
A Creative and Courageous Voice

66 *You may write me down in history,*
With your bitter, twisted lies,
You may trod me in the very dirt,
But still, like dust, I'll rise. 99
— Maya Angelou, "Still I Rise"

Life Portraits

MAYA ANGELOU
A Creative and Courageous Voice

By Jill Egan

Gareth Stevens
Publishing

Please visit our web site at **www.garethstevens.com.**
For a free catalog describing Gareth Stevens Publishing's list of high-quality books, call 1-800-542-2595 (USA) or 1-800-387-3178 (Canada).
Gareth Stevens Publishing's fax: 1-877-542-2596

Library of Congress Cataloging-in-Publication Data
Egan, Jill.
    Maya Angelou: a creative and courageous voice / by Jill Egan.
        p. cm. — (Life portraits)
      Includes bibliographical references and index.
      ISBN-10: 1-4339-0057-2   ISBN-13: 978-1-4339-0057-0 (lib. bdg.)
      1. Angelou, Maya.   2. Authors, American—20th century—Biography.
  3. African American women authors—Biography. I. Title.
PS3551.N464Z65   2009
818'.5409—dc22
  [B]   2008031542

This edition first published in 2009 by
Gareth Stevens Publishing
A Weekly Reader® Company
1 Reader's Digest Rd.
Pleasantville, NY 10570-7000 USA

Copyright © 2009 by Gareth Stevens, Inc.

Executive Managing Editor: Lisa M. Herrington
Creative Director: Lisa Donovan
Cover Designer: Keith Plechaty
Interior Designers: Yin Ling Wong and Keith Plechaty
Publisher: Keith Garton

Produced by Spooky Cheetah Press
www.spookycheetah.com
Editor: Stephanie Fitzgerald
Designer: Kimberly Shake
Cartographer: XNR Productions, Inc.
Proofreader: Jessica Cohn
Indexer: Madge Walls, All Sky Indexing

Printed in the United States of America

1 2 3 4 5 6 7 8 9 12 11 10 09 08

TABLE OF CONTENTS

In 1993, Maya Angelou secured her place in history.
She was the first African American, and the first
woman, to read a poem at a presidential inauguration.

CHAPTER ONE

AMERICA'S POET

THE SUN SHINED DOWN ON MAYA ANGELOU as she stood at the podium on the steps of the Capitol Building in Washington, D.C. The date was January 20, 1993. Maya was there for the inauguration of America's 42nd president, William Jefferson Clinton. She was about to read her poem "On the Pulse of Morning." She had written it especially for this occasion.

The 6-foot-tall, 64-year-old poet gazed out on a crowd of nearly 250,000 people. Millions more, she knew, would be watching on television at home. "I tried not to realize where I was," Maya remembers thinking at the moment. "I tried to suspend myself. I was afraid I might lose my composure." Maya may have been nervous, but it didn't show. She had worked on the poem for weeks. In some ways, she had been preparing for this moment for her entire life.

EARLY STRUGGLES

Maya grew up in what was known as the "Jim Crow" South. As with many African Americans of her generation, racism was a constant presence in Maya's life. Extra hardships were heaped on the little girl's shoulders, as well. When she was only 3 years old, Maya's parents sent her to live with her grandmother. She struggled with feelings of abandonment her whole life. When a family friend abused her at age 7, Maya stopped speaking for about five years.

Feelings of loneliness and inadequacy crowded the little girl's thoughts. At this difficult time in her early life, Maya found comfort in reading. Books and poems became her best friends. They helped her survive. It would be many years before Maya found her own voice through writing. A lifetime of experiences—as a dancer, an actress, a civil rights activist, and more—formed

Jim Crow Laws

Jim Crow laws were in place in the American South from 1876 until the Civil Rights Act was passed in 1964. The system called for a "separate but equal" policy for black and white people. Instead it ended up creating a society where black people experienced social, economic, and educational disadvantages. Under Jim Crow, black people were required to be separate from whites in schools, restaurants, buses, and anywhere else people might ordinarily come together.

the foundation for Maya's breakthrough book, *I Know Why the Caged Bird Sings.* The best-selling book, which told the story of Maya's early life, catapulted her to fame. Although Maya's book was representative of the African American experience, her words were universal. People from all walks of life were able to relate to the experiences of this remarkable woman. "It may be that Mr. Clinton asked me to write the inaugural poem because he understood that I am the kind of person who really does bring people together," Maya later realized.

> **"It may be that Mr. Clinton asked me to write the inaugural poem because he understood that I am the kind of person who really does bring people together."**
>
> – MAYA ANGELOU

AN INCREDIBLE INVITATION

Just days after he was elected, Clinton invited Maya to compose and read a poem for his inauguration. It was a great honor. Maya would be the first African American—and the first woman—to read a poem at an inauguration. It is amazing to think that someone who had been silent for so long had now been asked to speak for a nation.

Rarely at a loss for words, the writer was stunned speechless. She later recalled:

> *I thought of my grandmother ... and my grandfather ...*
> *and my great-grandmother who had been born a slave in*
> *Arkansas. I thought, how would those ancestors revel in*

such news? Their progeny (offspring) had been asked to participate at the highest level ... in the highest place in our country.

After Maya accepted Clinton's invitation, she quickly got to work. For weeks she struggled to find just the right words. Though she was writing her poem for the president, Maya knew that it would be heard by people around the world. She wanted to say something that spoke to everyone.

As Maya read her poem on that January morning, she spoke of hope and called for peace and brotherhood among all people.

President Clinton was thrilled with the poem Maya wrote for his inauguration. Over the years, the poet developed a friendship with the president and his wife.

An Award-Winning Poem

Maya's reading of "On the Pulse of Morning" was a triumph. People all over the country wanted copies of their own, so Maya created an audio version of the poem. In 1994, Maya's recording of "On the Pulse of Morning" won a Grammy Award for Best Spoken Word or Non-Musical Album. Originally called a "Gramophone Award," a Grammy is considered the highest honor in the United States recording and music industry.

President Clinton beamed with pride as the last lines of "On the Pulse of Morning" rang out:

Here on the pulse of this new day,
You may have the grace to look up and out
And into your sister's eyes,
And into your brother's face,
Your country,
And say simply
Very simply
With hope—
Good morning.

Maya's reading was greeted with thunderous applause. The once-silent girl had been transformed into one of history's most celebrated voices. ❖

By the time she was just 8 years old, Marguerite Johnson had already lived a complicated life.

CHAPTER TWO

A CHALLENGING CHILDHOOD

MAYA ANGELOU WAS BORN MARGUERITE ANN Johnson on April 4, 1928, in St. Louis, Missouri. Her parents divorced when she was 3 years old, and Marguerite and her brother, Bailey, were sent to live with their grandmother. Their father placed the children on a train bound for Stamps, Arkansas. A tag attached to Marguerite's wrist instructed that she and Bailey were to be delivered to their grandmother, Mrs. Annie Henderson.

Marguerite's grandmother was strict but very caring. The children loved their grandmother, whom they called "Momma," and felt welcome in her home from the start. Momma instructed the children to have good manners, to be respectful of adults, and to have faith in God. Their Uncle Willie, who also lived with Momma, was another source of comfort. He believed strongly in education and always encouraged the children to learn.

Marguerite's grandmother, Annie "Momma" Henderson, was a powerful influence on the young girl.

Despite the warmth of her new home, Marguerite felt abandoned by her parents. It was a feeling that would haunt her throughout her childhood. Her brother, Bailey, was her best friend and the only person who could understand her feelings of rejection.

Marguerite also found acceptance and understanding in the pages of books. In her readings, the little girl discovered characters with whom she could identify and writers who seemed to be speaking just to her. She enjoyed the work of black writers such as Langston Hughes and Paul Laurence Dunbar. She also had favorites among white writers, including William Shakespeare, Rudyard Kipling, and Charles Dickens. "They were my friends," she said of these authors.

DEALING WITH DISCRIMINATION

Marguerite's childhood difficulties were tied not only to her family problems. She was also dealing with the same intense racial discrimination experienced by all black people in the South. At the time, Jim Crow laws separated black and white people under a social and legal structure known as segregation. Black people were not treated equally or even fairly in much of the country. In the South racism was particularly strong. This was the land where slavery had its roots and where lynchings were committed all too often.

In Stamps, there were two sides of town—the black side and the white side. Black and white people went to different schools, different stores, they even walked along different roads. Momma ran the Wm. Johnson General Merchandise Store, the only general store in the black section of Stamps. This was the place where Marguerite lived and spent most of her time.

Lynching in America

During the years from 1882 to 1968, angry mobs took the law into their own hands. They lynched, or killed, an estimated 5,000 people. Hanging was the most common method of lynching. A majority of lynchings occurred in the South, and four out of five victims were black. In 2005, the United States Congress officially apologized for never having enacted an anti-lynching law.

The Wm. Johnson General Store in Stamps, Arkansas, is the place Marguerite called home—and where she spent most of her time as a child.

One afternoon, a former sheriff named Mr. Steward visited Momma's store. He told the family that a black man had bothered a white woman. He warned them that Uncle Willie might receive a visit from members of the Ku Klux Klan (KKK). Years later, Marguerite recalled the terror she felt. "Even after the slow drag of years, I remember the sense of fear which filled my mouth with hot, dry air, and made my body light," she wrote.

Uncle Willie hadn't done anything wrong, but he was still in danger. If members of the KKK were looking to attack a black man, it wouldn't matter which one they found. Anyone in the wrong place at the wrong time could be killed.

Uncle Willie hid in a bin used to hold onions and potatoes. Throughout the long, agonizing night, the family listened to Uncle Willie's fearful moans from inside the bin. The KKK never came calling that night. Looking back, however, Marguerite still believes that if they had come to the store, "They would have surely found Uncle Willie and just as surely lynched him."

> "I remember the sense of fear which filled my mouth with hot, dry air, and made my body light."
>
> — MAYA ANGELOU

AN ALIEN LIFE

Marguerite and her family had very few dealings with whites. Many years later, she recalled:

In Stamps the segregation was so complete that most Black children didn't really, absolutely know what whites looked like. Other than that they were different, to be dreaded, and in that dread was included the hostility of the powerless against the powerful, the poor against the rich, the worker against the worked for and the ragged against the well dressed.

Although she rarely saw them, Marguerite knew certain things about white people. She knew that white children had a different, easier life—and that they lived by different rules.

Marguerite had her first real brush with discrimination at the movies. A white girl was selling tickets. When Marguerite gave the girl a dime for her ticket, the girl refused to touch the

The Ku Klux Klan

The Ku Klux Klan (KKK) was formed in Tennessee around 1866 by a group of Confederate Army veterans. Members of the Klan, who often wore white robes and hoods to hide their identities, terrorized minorities, particularly black people. Klan members used many methods to intimidate their victims, including burning crosses in black people's yards or throwing rocks through their windows. They also tortured and murdered many black people during the early and middle parts of the 20th century. Historically, Klan membership was strongest in the South.

money. Instead, she used a card to push the dime into the change box. Then she refused to give Marguerite or Bailey a ticket. She wouldn't even speak to them. She just flicked her hand in the direction of the theater entrance. It was the first time Marguerite realized she was being treated badly because of the color of her skin. She decided at that moment she would boycott the movies. This would be Marguerite's first act as a civil rights activist. It would not be her last.

LONGING FOR ACCEPTANCE

For the three years that Marguerite and Bailey lived in Stamps, they did not hear anything from their parents. Momma told them that their parents lived in "a heaven called California, where ... they could have all the oranges they could eat. And the sun shone all the time," Marguerite later wrote. "I was sure that wasn't so. I couldn't believe that our mother would laugh and eat oranges in the sunshine without her children." In fact, Marguerite had convinced herself that her mother was dead. "I could cry anytime I wanted by picturing my mother (I didn't quite know what she looked like) lying in her coffin," she recalled years later. The little girl was amazed—and hurt to receive Christmas presents from her parents in 1934. It was proof that her parents were alive—and that they hadn't bothered to contact her before.

> "I couldn't believe that our mother would laugh and eat oranges in the sunshine without her children."
>
> – MAYA ANGELOU

No matter how bad she felt, there was one person whose love Marguerite never doubted. Her brother Bailey always protected her and made her feel wanted. Years later, she wrote about her feelings for Bailey:

Of all the needs (there are none imaginary) a lonely child has, the one that must be satisfied, if there is going to be hope and a hope of wholeness, is the unshaking need for an unshakable God. My pretty Black brother was my Kingdom Come.

REUNITING WITH HER PARENTS

One morning in 1935, when Marguerite was 7 years old, a sparkling gray car pulled up outside Momma's store. Marguerite's father, Bailey Johnson, had come to visit for three weeks. Marguerite's world was turned upside down when Johnson asked his children to go with him when he left Stamps. They were going to St. Louis, Missouri, to see their mother.

When Marguerite first saw her mother, she thought she'd discovered why she and Bailey had been sent away. "She was too beautiful to have children," Marguerite remembers thinking. A few days later, their father left without explanation. Once again, Marguerite felt betrayed and abandoned.

> **"[Mother] was like a pretty kite that floated just above my head."**
>
> – MAYA ANGELOU

For several months, Bailey and Marguerite stayed with their mother's family, the Baxters. The family was a tough and rowdy bunch—the opposite of Momma and Uncle Willie. Grandmother Baxter was a pale-skinned woman who spoke with a German accent and commanded respect. The six Baxter children, including Marguerite's mother Vivian, were known for being mean and quick-tempered.

Marguerite didn't see her mother much. Sometimes the children met Vivian at a tavern. "While we sat on the stiff wooden booths, Mother would dance alone in front of us to music from the [jukebox]," Marguerite later wrote. "I loved her most at those times. She was like a pretty kite that floated just above my head."

Taverns called speakeasies were popular in the mid-1930s. Marguerite's mother often met friends at a local speakeasy like the one shown here.

While her home life in St. Louis was unusual at best, Marguerite found some sense of balance in school. Uncle Willie and Momma's strictness about studying had paid off. "We were moved up a grade because our teachers thought that we country children would make our classmates feel inferior—and we did," Marguerite later explained.

After about six months, Marguerite and Bailey left their grandparents' house. They moved in with their mother and her boyfriend, Mr. Freeman. One morning when no one was home, Mr. Freeman sexually abused Marguerite. Afterward, he threatened the little girl. He said that if she ever told anyone what happened, he would kill Bailey.

A YOUNG VOICE SILENCED

Marguerite was scared and confused. She didn't say anything to her brother, and there was no one else to tell. Bailey had an active social life, but Marguerite hadn't made any friends in St. Louis. The books she checked out from the library were Marguerite's only company.

A few months later, in the late spring of 1935, Marguerite found herself alone in the house with Freeman again. This time, her mother's boyfriend raped her. She was 7 years old. Once again, Freeman threatened to kill Bailey if Marguerite told anyone what happened.

Marguerite felt sick and stayed in bed for several days. Freeman had moved out of the house, but Marguerite was still too scared to tell her mother what was wrong. Eventually the little girl shared her terrible secret with her brother.

Bailey was a year older than Marguerite. He offered support and guidance to his younger sister throughout her life.

Mr. Freeman was arrested and placed on trial. A brave Marguerite testified against him. Freeman was sentenced to a year and a day in prison, but was released later that same day.

A few days later, a policeman visited the house. Marguerite listened in while Grandma Baxter talked to the officer. He said that Freeman had been found kicked to death. The news hit Marguerite like a hurricane. She blamed herself for Freeman's death. She believed that her words in court had caused him to die. She began to worry that if she spoke again, someone else might die.

For about five years, Marguerite didn't speak to anyone except Bailey. For a few weeks, the Baxter family overlooked Marguerite's strange, self-induced condition. When the doctor said Marguerite had healed physically, the family began to see her silence as a sign of disrespect. They punished the little girl and tried to get her to speak by hitting her. Marguerite refused. Frustrated by her behavior, Vivian sent Marguerite and Bailey back to Stamps. Marguerite was deeply wounded, but her loss would soon be repaid many times over. In silence, the voiceless girl would discover the power of words. She would also find a rare ability to understand the rhythm and meaning of life. ❖

As a young woman, Marguerite struggled to find acceptance. Reclaiming her voice proved to be one of her most important achievements.

CHAPTER THREE

FINDING HER VOICE

T HE QUIET OF STAMPS WAS EXACTLY WHAT
Marguerite needed. At home with Momma and Uncle
Willie, she found some peace. Everyone in the com-
munity accepted her silence as a sign of her "tender-hearted"
nature. No one pushed her to speak. Bailey was the only person
Marguerite communicated with at all.

Ever since Marguerite stopped speaking, she had become
more enchanted with language. She read as much as she could.
She memorized her favorite poems. Like a photographer cap-
tures a scene, she took the words in and held them in her mind
like a picture. While she walked alone through the dusty streets
of Stamps or sat quietly and unnoticed in the shadow of the
store, Marguerite would pull up the poems. She would play the
words of Shakespeare, Dunbar, and others over and over to keep
herself company.

BRINGING WORDS TO LIFE

Marguerite also started writing when she returned to Stamps. Every day the young girl filled a journal with essays and poetry. It was a safe place to express the things she wasn't willing to say out loud. The hurt of abuse and abandonment wounded her, but writing gave Marguerite a way to begin to heal. She dreamed that one day her poems would be published and read aloud. For a black girl in the South, that dream had little chance of becoming a reality.

Marguerite remained alone in her silence until a woman in the community helped her find her voice again. Her name was Bertha Flowers. "She was one of the few gentlewomen I have ever known," Marguerite said later, "and has remained throughout my life the measure of what a human being can be."

> **"Words mean more than what is set down on paper. It takes the human voice to infuse them with the shades of deeper meaning."**
>
> – BERTHA FLOWERS

One day, Mrs. Flowers asked Marguerite to help carry her groceries home. As they walked, she talked to Marguerite about the power of the spoken word. She commended the young girl for reading, but added that reading alone wasn't good enough. "Words mean more than what is set down on paper," she explained. "It takes the human voice to infuse them with the shades of deeper meaning."

When they arrived at her house, Mrs. Flowers read to Marguerite from *A Tale of Two Cities* by Charles Dickens. Marguerite had read the story before. When she heard it read

Charles Dickens

British author Charles Dickens (1812–1870) is considered one of the greatest writers of the 19th century. His novels and short stories remain among the most popular books of all time. Known for his fascinating characters and plots, Dickens introduced the world to Ebenezer Scrooge and the phrase, "Bah, humbug," in *A Christmas Carol* (1843). His other stories, *A Tale of Two Cities* (1859), *Great Expectations* (1861), and *David Copperfield* (1850) are still widely read and have been turned into numerous stage and film productions. His words inspired Maya Angelou to find her voice and develop her skills as a writer.

aloud, however, she wondered if the words could possibly be the same. When Mrs. Flowers finished, she asked Marguerite if she liked the story. The child broke her silence with a simple reply. "Yes ma'am," she said. Years later, Marguerite reflected on her response. "It was the least I could do, but it was the most also."

Though it would be four more years until she fully reclaimed her voice, Mrs. Flowers had sparked something in the young girl.

HARD LESSONS LEARNED

Marguerite was regaining her voice and her confidence. Soon, however, several cruel racist incidents would make it impossible for her and Bailey to remain in Stamps.

In 1940, when she was 12 years old, Marguerite graduated from the eighth grade. The days leading up to the ceremony at Lafayette County Training School were filled with excitement and pride. As she sat in the audience on graduation day, however, Marguerite's happy feelings were nearly shattered. Mr. Edward Donleavy, a white school official from Texarkana, got up to speak. He told the audience all about how the white students at Central School would be future inventors, artists, and scientists. Then he went on to praise the athleticism of the boys at

Becoming an athlete, such as Olympic Gold Medal winner Jesse Owens, was considered by some to be the biggest success an African American could achieve.

Marguerite's school. These boys, Donleavy suggested, could try to be the next athletic heroes like boxer Joe Louis or Olympic Gold Medal winner Jesse Owens. Donleavy didn't mention the Lafayette girls at all.

"The man's dead words fell like bricks around the auditorium and too many settled in my belly," Marguerite remembered. The words were like poison to the people in the audience. One by one, heads in the crowd began to lower. Everyone tried to avoid looking at the man who was lobbing insults at them.

The message behind Donleavy's words was clear: Black people could never hope to be anything more than maids, farmers, or athletes. "It was brutal to be young and already trained to sit quietly and listen to charges brought against my color with no chance of defense," Marguerite later recalled.

Later in the ceremony, Marguerite's classmate Henry Reed delivered his valedictorian speech. Then he did something unexpected. He began to sing the poem "Lift Ev'ry Voice and Sing," by James Weldon Johnson. It was a song Marguerite had sung many, many times, but this time, she really heard the words—and so did the others in the room.

> **"It was brutal to be young and already trained to sit quietly and listen to charges brought against my color with no chance of defense."**
>
> – MAYA ANGELOU

"The tears that slipped down many faces were not wiped away in shame," Marguerite noticed. "We were on top again. As always, again. We survived," she thought with a sense of pride.

Lift Ev'ry Voice

"Lift Ev'ry Voice and Sing" is often called the "Black National Anthem." The second verse provides a good example of why this poem meant so much to black people in America:

Stony the road we trod,
Bitter the chast'ning rod,
Felt in the days when hope unborn had died;
Yet, with a steady beat,
Have not our weary feet,
Come to the place for which our fathers sighed?
We have come over a way that with tears has
    been watered,
We have come, treading our path through the blood
    of the slaughtered,
Out from the gloomy past,
Till now we stand at last
Where the white gleam of our bright star is cast.

The words of Dickens and Dunbar helped Marguerite survive her childhood heartbreak and reclaim her voice. Now the words of James Weldon Johnson were helping the black community survive the ignorance and harshness of a racist society.

Nevertheless, an ugly pattern was becoming clear to the young girl. Time after time white people would knock black people down. Time after time, black people would pick themselves up. Then, one year after her graduation, Marguerite's will to pick herself up again was sorely tested.

Because of the Jim Crow laws, there were separate dentists for black and white people. The closest black dentist was 25 miles (40 kilometers) away, however, and 13-year-old Marguerite had a terrible toothache. Momma decided to take Marguerite to Dr. Lincoln, the white dentist, who was right in Stamps. This was an emergency—Marguerite was in terrible pain. Besides, Momma said the white dentist owed her a favor. During the Great Depression 10 years before, Momma had lent Dr. Lincoln money. Surely, the dentist would return the act of kindness.

Throughout the Jim Crow South, African Americans were forced to use separate public facilities, such as water fountains that were marked "Colored."

Momma was in for a rude awakening. Dr. Lincoln refused to treat Marguerite. "I'd rather stick my hand in a dog's mouth," he said. Marguerite was hurt, and Momma was angry. There was nothing they could do, however, except take comfort from each other. Marguerite sat close to Momma on the long bus ride to the black dentist's office.

Marguerite moved around a lot as a child. By the time she was 15, she'd lived in St. Louis, Stamps—twice—and California.

On a hot, sticky summer day in 1941, 16-year-old Bailey came into the store looking shaken. He had just returned from an errand to the white part of town where he had witnessed a black man's body being pulled out of the lake. Bailey suspected that members of the KKK had killed the man and dumped him in the water. That incident was

> **"I'd rather stick my hand in a dog's mouth."**
>
> – DR. LINCOLN

the last straw. Momma feared for Bailey's safety. Marguerite's older brother had developed into a self-confident young man with a sharp tongue. In the South, a black man like Bailey was in danger of meeting the same fate as the man in the lake. Within a few weeks, the children were headed to California, where their mother now lived.

A FRESH START

Marguerite was nervous about seeing her mother again. Vivian was nervous, too. These shared emotions helped mother and daughter connect and begin to form a loving relationship.

Soon after Marguerite and Bailey arrived in California, their mother married Daddy Clidell. Clidell was a simple, good, and honest man. He was the first father figure Marguerite ever knew. In early 1942, the family settled in San Francisco in a 14-room home that they shared with a series of boarders.

Marguerite enrolled at an all girls' high school near her home. Because of her good grades in Stamps, Marguerite was moved up a grade in school. She was not happy, though. The girls were tougher and more prejudiced than she was used to. Many of the black girls were like Marguerite and had just moved from the South. Unlike Marguerite, "They strutted with an aura of invincibility, and … they absolutely intimidated the white girls and those Black and Mexican students who had no shield of fearlessness." After just a few weeks, Vivian transferred Marguerite to another school.

For the first semester, Marguerite was one of only three black students in the new school. For the first time in her life, she was not the brightest student. The white students, she found, had better vocabularies and less fear in the classroom. "They never hesitated to hold up their hands in response to a teacher's question;" she later recalled, "even if they were wrong they were wrong aggressively, while I had to be certain about all my facts before I dared to call attention to myself."

San Francisco in the early 1940s was different from Stamps, Arkansas. The harsh, dangerous racism of the South was less of a problem in this bustling city.

A lucky break would soon help Marguerite overcome her fear of being noticed. She never discovered why, but when she was 14, Marguerite received a scholarship to attend night classes at college. She enrolled in drama and dance classes, which would provide future career opportunities. Her drama experience would also come into play when she found her

"Even if [the white students] were wrong they were wrong aggressively, while I had to be certain about all my facts before I dared to call attention to myself."

— MAYA ANGELOU

ultimate calling as a writer. Marguerite's drama training surely strengthened her famed ability to make language come alive.

A VISIT WITH DADDY BAILEY

In 1943, when she was 15, Marguerite's father asked her to spend the summer in San Diego with him and his girlfriend, Dolores. A few weeks into the visit, Daddy Bailey planned a car trip to Mexico. He was crossing the border to buy groceries. When Daddy asked Marguerite to join him, she jumped at the chance.

Dolores was jealous that Bailey had taken Marguerite to Mexico instead of her. As soon as they returned, Dolores started a fight. "Bailey, you've let your children come between us," she said. The two argued until Bailey finally stormed out.

Once they were alone, Marguerite tried to smooth things over with Dolores. Her apology did nothing to pacify the woman, however. "Why don't you go back to your mother? If you've got one," Dolores screamed.

Marguerite was furious. This woman couldn't insult her mother! The teenager slapped Dolores. "She was out of the chair like a flea," Marguerite recalled, "and before I could jump back she had her arms around me."

Marguerite finally untangled herself from Dolores's grip and ran outside. She felt a wetness under her arm that she quickly realized was blood. Dolores had cut her. Now the woman was coming at her with a hammer. Marguerite locked herself in the car. When Daddy Bailey heard the commotion he came running.

As soon as he realized his daughter was bleeding, Daddy Bailey rushed Marguerite to a friend's home. After the wound was cleaned and bandaged, Bailey dropped his daughter off at another friend's house and returned to his girlfriend.

Once again feeling abandoned and let down, Marguerite ran away. She didn't know where to go. She had always heard it whispered that one of her uncles had killed Mr. Freeman. Now she was afraid that if she went home and told her mother what happened, the Baxter family might kill Dolores or Daddy Bailey. As she walked the streets of the city, she came upon a junkyard filled with abandoned cars. Marguerite searched until she found a clean car that was safe from rats. Then she hunkered down, said her prayers, and fell asleep.

> **"She was out of the chair like a flea, and before I could jump back she had her arms around me."**
>
> – MAYA ANGELOU

The next morning, Marguerite woke to find her car surrounded by a group of teenagers. They were watching her through the

Bailey Johnson had a gift for languages that he passed onto his daughter. He and Marguerite both spoke several languages.

windows. The faces were a mix of white, black, and Mexican. Marguerite could see they were laughing and talking but she couldn't hear their words. She prayed their laughter wasn't directed at her. When Marguerite opened her door, any worries she had fell away. The group immediately accepted her.

"After a month my thinking processes had so changed that I was hardly recognizable to myself," she later recalled. "The unquestioning acceptance by my peers had dislodged the familiar insecurity." Here at the junkyard, the color of one's skin meant nothing. For the first time, Marguerite experienced the feeling of being accepted as part of a community. Still, after four weeks, she was ready to go home to her mother. Vivian sent Marguerite a train ticket home without question. It would be years until Marguerite shared the entire story with her family. ❖

Marguerite had many artistic talents in addition to writing. She was also an accomplished dancer and a popular singer.

CHAPTER FOUR

CREATING MAYA ANGELOU

W HEN WORLD WAR II ENDED IN 1945, MANY people lost their jobs. Men and women who had moved to California for work were heading home. The boarders that once filled the rooms of Daddy Clidell's house were leaving. Soon the whole family was feeling the financial strain. The addition of another mouth to feed added an extra burden. Days after she graduated from high school, 17-year-old Marguerite gave birth to a son whom she named Clyde.

Two months later, Marguerite moved out. She was determined to support her baby on her own. She worked odd jobs to make ends meet. Nothing was beneath Marguerite, who worked as a Creole cook and peeled paint off cars with her bare hands. Supporting herself and her son was more difficult than the young mother had anticipated, however. Desperate for money, she briefly turned to prostitution.

Marguerite realized the life she was living went against everything she had been taught as a child. Though she was only 19 years old, she was mature enough to realize she had to make a change. "It is wise to take the time to develop one's own way of being, increasing those things one does well and eliminating the elements in one's character which can hinder and diminish the good personality," she later explained. Marguerite ran back to the safety of Stamps—and Momma and Uncle Willie.

Marguerite was glad for the comfort of home. It quickly became clear, however, that she could not stay in Stamps. She was used to living in a more equal society. Segregation and racism in Stamps were as bad as they had been in her childhood. Marguerite refused to move backward and she refused to subject her son to the same racism she had experienced. After just a few months, Marguerite and Clyde returned to San Francisco.

Marguerite went back to working as a cook and eventually found a job at a record store. In 1951, Marguerite fell in love with one of the customers, Enistasious (Tosh) Angelos. Vivian was not happy when Tosh proposed to her daughter. Marguerite's mother disapproved of the young man who was both white and poor. Although they would be allowed to marry in California, interracial relationships were frowned

> **"It is wise to take the time to develop one's own way of being, increasing those things one does well and eliminating the elements in one's character which can hinder and diminish the good personality."**
>
> – MAYA ANGELOU

Uncle Willie (right, with a neighborhood friend) always encouraged Marguerite to work hard for success.

upon—and even illegal—in many states at the time. Bailey, always Marguerite's strongest supporter, encouraged his sister to follow her heart. Vivian showed her displeasure by leaving town right before her daughter's wedding.

Marguerite spent the first year of her marriage cooking gourmet meals and keeping the house spotless. For a short time, her desire to be the perfect wife masked the growing unhappiness and loneliness she was feeling. In an attempt to feel better about herself, Marguerite applied for and won a scholarship to a dance school in New York City. She, Tosh, and Clyde moved to the East Coast for a year. By the time the family returned to San Francisco in 1953, Marguerite had made two decisions: She wanted a divorce, and she wanted to be a dancer.

FOLLOWING A DREAM

Once again, Marguerite had to make her own way in the world. This time, however, she wanted a career that meant something to her. She found a job performing at a nightclub called The Garden of Allah. One of Marguerite's many fans was Jorie Remus, a singer who worked at the famous late-night cabaret called The Purple Onion.

Jorie complained to Marguerite about always being asked to sing Calypso music. Marguerite said that she loved Calypso music—especially the stories the lyrics told. After a late-night, impromptu audition at a party at Jorie's apartment, Marguerite was offered a job singing Calypso music at The Purple Onion. There was just one problem: her name. Marguerite Johnson was not considered exotic enough. It was time for a change.

Calypso Music

Calypso music is said to have originated in Trinidad around 1900. Its roots go back to the years when Africans were carried across the Atlantic Ocean in slave ships, however. Slaves were not allowed to speak to each other, so they found a different way to communicate—through song. Calypso lyrics can be about anything from relationships to small town scandals to world politics. The songs are generally a way to spread news and stories. It's no wonder Marguerite found the music so appealing.

When they were growing up, Bailey refused to call his sister by her given name. Instead, he called her "Mya Sister." Gradually, the nickname became "Maya." Marguerite thought the nickname might be right for a stage name. Her friends at The Purple Onion agreed. A slight adjustment was then made to her married name of Angelos, and Maya Angelou was born.

A RISING STAR

One night in 1954, Maya went to the theater to see the traveling production of *Porgy and Bess.* The opera, a love story set in the slums of Charleston, South Carolina, had started out on Broadway. It had finally made its way to San Francisco. By the time the second act began, Maya was mesmerized. The singing and dancing were the most moving performances she had ever seen. When a solo dancer took the stage, Maya thought she had found her calling. She wanted to be that dancer.

A few nights later, some of the *Porgy and Bess* cast saw Maya perform at The Purple Onion. They applauded her performance and she, in turn, applauded them. After becoming friendly with the cast, Maya was invited to audition for the show. She won the part, but Maya had two months left on her contract with The Purple Onion. The manager would not let her out of it. The *Porgy and Bess* cast left San Francisco a few weeks later. Maya took voice lessons and continued performing at The Purple Onion, but thoughts of *Porgy and Bess* wouldn't disappear.

Three days before her contract at The Purple Onion was set to expire, Maya was asked to audition for a new Broadway show called *House of Flowers.* Maya left Clyde with her mother and was on a plane to New York days later. She won the part after just one audition. Maya was still flying high from the news when the phone rang. Bob Dustin, a manager from *Porgy and Bess*, was calling to offer her the role of principal dancer in the traveling production. Maya accepted the part, leaving Broadway behind without a second thought.

Only one thing marred this perfect moment. Maya would have to go directly from New York to Montreal to join the cast. There would be no time to go back to San Francisco to say good-bye to Clyde. Maya was torn. She had never forgotten her own feelings of abandonment when she was a child. "I did not relish visiting the same anguish on my son," she said. Family and friends convinced Maya that Clyde would be fine, and she vowed to herself that she would make it up to him someday. Over the phone, she promised her son that she would be home soon—even though she knew she would likely be away for nearly two years.

Maya toured Italy, France, Egypt, Israel, Yugoslavia (now Serbia and Montenegro), and Greece with *Porgy and Bess*. Maya was able to see the world while performing with people she admired in a role she adored. She was also learning what it was like to live in a world that was free from the racism of the segregated United States. She was experiencing a new sense of freedom—and she liked the way it felt.

HOMEWARD BOUND

After a year on the road, Maya received a letter from her mother. Clyde needed her. Maya wanted to leave immediately, but it took her two months to earn the money for the fare back home.

Maya visited the ruins at Pompeii in Italy with the cast of Porgy and Bess. *She frolicked with the children to keep them from looking at the sometimes grisly remains.*

When she arrived in San Francisco, Maya found that Clyde was no longer the energetic little boy she had left behind. He had grown into a quiet 9-year-old who avoided eye contact with his mother and clung to her fiercely. "When are you going away again?" he asked.

> **"I swear to you, I'll never leave you again."**
>
> – MAYA ANGELOU TO HER SON

Maya's heart sank. "I put my arms around him and he fell sobbing on my chest. I held him, but not my own tears," she recalled. "I swear to you, I'll never leave you again," Maya vowed. "If I go, when I go, you'll go with me or I won't go."

Maya kept her promise. For the next few years, mother and son lived in California, New York, Ohio, and Hawaii as Maya pursued singing jobs in various nightclubs. As Clyde regained his confidence in his relationship with his mother he became more independent. He was just 10 years old when he announced that he was changing his name to Guy.

Maya and her son settled in Los Angeles in 1956. It was perfect timing. Calypso music was bigger than ever, and Maya was a budding star. In 1957, she made her movie debut in the musical *Calypso Heat Wave*. Later that year, she recorded the album *Miss Calypso*. Maya had achieved great success as a singer and could have had a brilliant career. However, she knew that singing was not her true calling.

Maya adored words and language. She had always kept a journal filled with her poems and songs. Until this point in her life, she had always thought of writing as just a hobby. It had never occurred to her that it could be her career. While she was in Los Angeles, she rediscovered the passion for words she'd had as a child. She later remembered:

> *I began to write. At first I limited myself to short sketches, then to song lyrics, then I dared short stories. When I met John Killens he had just come to Hollywood to write the screenplay for his novel* Youngblood, *and he agreed to read some of what he called my 'work in progress.' I had written and recorded six songs for Liberty Records, but I didn't seriously think of writing until John gave me his critique. After that I thought of little else.*

Maya released an album, Miss Calypso, *in 1957. Even though she found success as a singer, Maya knew this was not her true calling. She was meant to write.*

Killens told Maya that her work needed rewriting and polishing. He also told her she had talent. He encouraged Maya to move to New York City and join the Harlem Writers Guild, which he had helped establish. She followed his advice. In 1959, Maya and 14-year-old Guy moved to Brooklyn, New York. She was ready to devote herself to writing full time. ❖

When Maya moved to New York City in 1959, she became passionate about writing—and the fight for civil rights.

CHAPTER FIVE

NEW DIRECTIONS

A S SOON AS SHE ARRIVED IN NEW YORK, MAYA attended her first meeting of the Harlem Writers Guild. She sat in on three meetings before it was her turn to read her own work out loud.

The group was filled with tough critics. Maya's heart raced as she started reading from her play *One Love. One Life.* "The blood pounded in my ears but not enough to drown the skinny sound of my voice," she remembers. "My hands shook so that I had to lay the pages in my lap, but that was not a good solution due to the tricks my knees were playing."

Guild member John Henrik Clarke had a reputation for being a tough but intelligent critic. Maya feared his reaction the most. As luck would have it, he offered his criticism first. "*One Life. One Love?* I found no life and very little love in the play from the opening of the act to its unfortunate end," he said.

Clarke softened his criticism by telling Maya he was glad to have her in the group. He also told her to go back to her piece and rework every sentence.

Maya was committed to developing and honing her writing skills, but she had to find a way to support herself and her son while she worked on her writing. She went back to singing in nightclubs and was booked at the famed Apollo Theater in Harlem for one week. Maya's performance of a Swahili song about freedom got the entire crowd singing. At the time, freedom was something almost everyone could sing about.

Police often used violent methods to break up civil rights protests. Sometimes they set dogs on black activists, other times they sprayed them with powerful firehoses.

A NEW CALLING

Maya and her son had arrived in New York just as the civil rights movement was starting to heat up. While the North wasn't officially segregated like the South, black people were still treated differently than whites. People across the country were demanding equal rights for black people. Sit-ins, boycotts, and other demonstrations were increasingly common.

Maya was determined to take part in the fight. She got the chance one summer night in 1960. That evening, Maya and her friend Godfrey Cambridge went to a Harlem church to hear Martin Luther King Jr. speak. King spoke powerfully about the suffering of his black brothers and sisters in the South. Maya remembers his message plainly:

> We, the black people, the most displaced, the poorest, the most maligned and scourged, we had the glorious task of reclaiming the soul and saving the honor of the country. We, the most hated, must take hate into our hands and by the miracle of love, turn loathing into love. We, the most feared and apprehensive, must take fear and by love, change it into hope.

King's words moved many in the congregation to tears. Maya and her friend were moved to action. They knew they must do something to help his cause. Maya put her writing on hold.

Maya and Godfrey put on a show featuring black performers to raise money for the Southern Christian Leadership Conference (SCLC). *Cabaret for Freedom* played to packed houses in New York City for more than a month in the summer of 1960.

Martin Luther King Jr.

Martin Luther King Jr. (1929–1968) was a Baptist preacher and one of the best-known and most admired leaders of the civil rights movement. Just as he inspired Maya Angelou, King moved thousands of people—black and white—to work together for equality. In 1964, Dr. King was awarded the Nobel Prize for Peace, becoming the youngest person ever to hold the honor. His efforts helped change race relations in the United States and helped get the 1964 Civil Rights Act passed. Today, King is remembered as a symbol of the civil rights movement, as well as a worldwide figure for freedom.

Maya's work on the cabaret caught the attention of Bayard Rustin, the director of the SCLC in New York. Rustin was planning to give up his position, and he wanted Maya to take over for him that fall. Placing her career as an entertainer and writer on hold, Maya accepted the position as the SCLC's Northeastern Regional Coordinator.

After working at the SCLC for two months, Maya returned from lunch one day to find King sitting in her office. "He was shorter than I expected," she recalled, "and so young. He had an easy friendliness, which was unsettling. Looking at him in my office, alone, was like seeing a lion sitting down at my dining-room eating a plate of mustard greens."

King was there to thank Maya in person for all her hard work. As they talked, King asked about her family and about her life in the South. Maya had admired him before, but he gained her affection for life when he asked about Bailey. At the time, Bailey was in prison for selling stolen goods. Instead of judging Maya or her brother, King offered her sympathy and support. "I understand," King said. "Disappointment drives our young men to some desperate lengths. That's why we must fight and win. We must save the Baileys of the world. And Maya, never stop loving him. Never give up on him. Never deny him. And remember, he is freer than those who hold him behind bars."

The Southern Christian Leadership Conference (SCLC)

The SCLC was founded in 1957 to coordinate the efforts of local protest groups in the South. Its president, Martin Luther King Jr., insisted that all SCLC-led protests must be nonviolent. The group often used boycotts and sit-ins to grab the attention of the nation—and lawmakers. The efforts of the SCLC helped bring about passage of the Civil Rights Act of 1964 and the Voting Rights Act of 1965.

There was a knock on the door, and King was whisked away. Maya sat and thought about her brief meeting with King. That day, she became even more committed to the fight for freedom.

FREEDOM FIGHTER

As she worked on the civil rights movement in America, Maya became increasingly concerned about the rights of people all over the world. The anti-apartheid, African freedom movement was just one of the other human rights causes Maya supported.

In the fall of 1960, 32-year-old Maya met a man who would change her life. Vusumzi (Vus) Make (pronounced Mah-kay) was a South African freedom fighter. He worked to end colonialism in Africa and to give black Africans equal human rights. Maya thought Vus was the most impressive person she'd ever met. His

Apartheid

Apartheid, the South African government's policy of segregation, was implemented in 1948. People were classified by color, with the white minority ruling the nonwhite majority. Segregation was enforced in every area of life, including housing, education, and transportation. In the 1980s and '90s, the South African government came under increasing pressure to end apartheid. The policy was officially reversed in 1991, though nonwhites continued to face racism and discrimination.

Maya and the South African anti-apartheid leader, Vus Make (center), were active in the fight for equal rights for all people.

brains, experience, and mission made him the ideal man in her eyes. Vus shared Maya's feelings, and soon asked her to marry him. After receiving her son's blessing, Maya and Vus began their life together, though they were never officially married.

Vus did not want Maya to work, so she resigned from the SCLC. When the family moved into their apartment in Manhattan, Maya settled into her new role as a homemaker. Still, she found time to continue her work as an activist. In 1961, she and some friends formed the Cultural Association for Women of African Heritage (CAWAH). The CAWAH was active in supporting human rights both in the United States and in Africa.

On January 17, 1961, Patrice Lumumba, the first prime minister of the newly independent Republic of the Congo, was assassinated. Lumumba was a leader in the anti-apartheid movement, and his death hit the freedom fighters hard. "We had been abused, and so long abused," Maya explained, "that the loss of one hero was a setback of such proportion it could dishearten us and weaken the struggle."

A few days later Maya and her friend Rosa Guy went to hear Malcolm X speak in Harlem. Malcolm and the Nation of Islam, the organization that he represented, held different views from Martin Luther King and the SCLC. King believed in equality and integration. The Nation of Islam believed that blacks should be politically, economically, and socially separate and independent from whites. Malcolm told the crowd, "Every person under the sound of my voice is a soldier. You are either fighting for your freedom or betraying the fight for freedom." The audience went

Maya and Rosa Guy (left) became close friends at the Harlem Writers Guild. They were both vocal activists in the civil rights movement.

wild. They were angry at being denied equality and freedom. Finally someone understood that anger.

"The Muslim tirade was just what we needed to hear," Maya later recalled. "Malcolm's words were harsh, but too close to the bitter truth to argue. Our people were alone. As always, alone. We could not expect protection from whites even if they happened to be our relatives."

Feeling that the CAWAH had to act to protest Lumumba's assassination, Maya and Rosa organized what was supposed to be a small demonstration at the United Nations. Instead, thousands of protesters showed up, and the demonstration quickly got out of control. The protest made headlines and caught the attention of Malcolm X. He told the press that he and other Muslims did not support the actions of the CAWAH.

> **"I had never been so affected by a human presence. Watching Malcolm X on television or even listening to him speak on a podium had been no preparation for meeting him face to face."**
>
> – MAYA ANGELOU

Maya and Rosa went to see Malcolm to find out what they had done wrong. The women were nervous as they walked into the office. "I had never been so affected by a human presence," Maya recalled. "Watching Malcolm X on television or even listening to him speak on a podium had been no preparation for meeting him face to face."

Malcolm's hair was redder than they had imagined, and his eyes were piercing. "You were wrong in your direction," he

Malcolm X

Malcolm X (1925–1965) was born Malcolm Little in Omaha, Nebraska. His father was an early civil rights activist whose efforts led the family to be targeted by white supremacists.

Malcolm was a close follower of the Nation of Islam and its leader, Elijah Muhammad. Followers of the Nation of Islam believed that black people and white people could never coexist peacefully. Malcolm became disillusioned by Elijah's behavior, however, and ultimately left the organization.

While on a pilgrimage to Mecca in 1964, Malcolm X changed his way of thinking. He no longer believed separation of the races was the solution. When he returned from his trip, Malcolm X founded the Muslim Mosque, Inc. and the Organization for Afro-American Unity. Maya Angelou was supposed to help him take the cause of black freedom and equality to the United Nations. Before she could do that, tragedy struck. On February 21, 1965 Malcolm X was gunned down in front of his family as he delivered a speech in New York City.

said looking straight into their eyes. "The people of Harlem are angry. And they have reason to be angry. But going to the United Nations, shouting and carrying placards will not win freedom for anyone." He explained that Muslims did not believe in demonstrations because they didn't accomplish anything.

Malcolm's disapproval of their efforts stung. The two women left the meeting feeling very discouraged. Maya even put her activism on hold for awhile. She got back into action in the spring of 1961 when an opportunity arose to take part in *The Blacks*. The play by Jean Genet was a satire about race and power. Unfortunately, problems with the production forced Maya to quit after several months.

> "The people of Harlem are angry. And they have reason to be angry. But ... shouting and carrying placards will not win freedom for anyone."
>
> – MALCOLM X

Things were not going much better at home. Vus spent money wildly and refused to discuss the family's financial situation with Maya. Instead, he announced that the family was relocating to Cairo, Egypt. Maya was moving to Africa, the land of her ancestors. ❖

During Maya's time in Africa, she learned more about being courageous and about the power and importance of freedom.

CHAPTER SIX

FINDING HOME IN AFRICA

WHEN MAYA'S PLANE TOUCHED DOWN IN Cairo, it was a homecoming of sorts. She and Guy were joining Vus and the other black Americans who had resettled in Africa. She was also connecting with her ancestors who had lived on the continent generations before.

Vus had prepared the apartment ahead of time and was happy to see his family. Guy quickly settled in. He'd made friends right away and was busy exploring Cairo. Vus traveled often for work, and Maya found that, once again, he was ignoring their finances. She decided to get a job.

Maya's friend David DuBois had been living in Cairo for several years. She asked David, who was the stepson of activist W.E.B. DuBois, for help. Although she didn't have any experience, David helped Maya get a job as an associate editor at the English-language magazine *The Arab Observer*.

W.E.B. DuBois

William Edward Burghardt DuBois (1868–1963) was born in Great Barrington, Massachusetts. The first African American to receive a Ph.D. from Harvard University, DuBois was a civil rights activist. He was also a founder of the National Association for the Advancement of Colored People (NAACP).

Maya worked at the magazine for about a year. During that time she established close friendships with two women, A. B. (Banti) Williamson, a Liberian, and Kebidetch Erdatchew, an Ethiopian. Banti and Kebidetch helped Maya adapt to her new life. They also offered her support when her relationship with Vus fell apart. By the spring of 1962, Maya and Vus had broken up. Still, Maya was happy with her life in Egypt.

During the summer of 1962, however, the mood in Cairo began to change. Tensions between Russia and the United States were threatening to start another world war. Anti-Americanism was rising in Egypt.

Maya started to feel unwelcome at *The Arab Observer*, and she resigned. Guy was graduating from high school and wanted to attend the University of Ghana. Once Guy left, Maya would be alone in Cairo. She decided to take a position at the Liberian Department of Information. Before she moved, Maya took her son to Accra, Ghana, to help him get settled at school.

The moment she stepped off the plane in Accra, Maya felt as if she'd arrived home. "We were Black Americans in West Africa, where for the first time in our lives the color of our skin was accepted as correct and normal," she explained.

In Accra, Maya and Guy stayed with a family friend who arranged for some South Africans and black Americans to visit. These visitors immediately embraced the duo and welcomed them to their country. One of the guests, Alice Windom, suggested that Maya meet other expatriates. The day after she arrived, Maya became reconnected with two of her friends from the Harlem Writers Guild—Julian Mayfield and his wife, Ana Livia Cordero.

In the early 1980s, Maya posed with her mother, Guy, and her grandson, Colin—who now has children of his own.

A CHANGE OF PLANS

Three days after they'd arrived in Accra, Guy was badly injured in a car accident. His neck was broken in three places, and an arm and a leg were fractured. He was lucky to be alive. Maya immediately canceled her plans to go to Liberia and stayed in Ghana to take care of her son.

Guy was in the hospital throughout July and August. Maya visited the hospital every day and brought home-cooked meals for her son. Her savings were dwindling, though. If she and Guy were going to survive, Maya would need to find work. She would also need to find courage. "Courage is the most important of all the virtues," she explains, "because without courage you can't practice any other virtue consistently."

Maya took an administrative job at the University of Ghana. A friend found a house she could stay in for free. Guy was recovering nicely, and Maya felt at home in Ghana. A renewed sense of hope filled her. "It was so wonderful to be in a country where nobody could complain that one was not given rights, or given promotion, because of one's color," she later explained.

After two months, Guy was well enough to enter the University of Ghana. Maya moved into a small bungalow with her friends Alice Windom and Vicki Garvin. To help pay the bills, she took on extra work writing for the *Ghanaian Times*.

Maya and her friends, who called themselves the Revolutionist Returnees, kept up on the news from the United States. When they heard about the March on Washington that was planned for August 28, 1963, they decided to hold their own march. They planned to march on the U.S. Embassy in Ghana at the same

The March on Washington for Jobs and Freedom

On August 28, 1963, more than 250,000 people gathered on the Mall in Washington, D.C. They were there to peacefully persuade Congress to pass civil rights legislation. There were many performances and speeches throughout the day, which reached a high point with Martin Luther King Jr.'s famous "I Have a Dream" speech. President John F. Kennedy was so impressed with the march—and with King's speech—that he invited the organizers to the White House to discuss the legislation. The Civil Rights Act was signed into law on July 2, 1964.

time on the same day. Their march in Ghana became even more meaningful when it turned into a tribute to W E.B. DuBois, who died on August 27.

RECONNECTING WITH MALCOLM X

At the end of April 1964, Malcolm X arrived in Accra. He had just returned from a pilgrimage to Mecca, the Muslim holy land. At a gathering at Julian Mayfield's home, Malcolm said the pilgrimage had changed him and his ideas. He no longer believed that all whites were "blue-eyed devils" or that any human being was born cruel. He had cut his ties to the Nation of Islam a month earlier on March 8, 1964. Now he courageously planned

Martin Luther King Jr. and a crowd of thousands urged Congress to pass civil rights legislation at the March on Washington on August 28, 1963. Maya and her friends in Ghana held their own march that day to show their support for King.

to make public statements that he knew would draw their anger. Malcolm told the group that he planned to take the case of black Americans to the United Nations. That way, he reasoned, the entire world could enter the debate. During this time, Maya and Malcolm developed a friendship that continued through letter writing after he left Ghana.

Meanwhile, Maya's relationship with her son was becoming strained. Guy had begun dating and wanted more independence. Maya knew she needed to give him space—and get some space herself. When she received a call asking her to appear in *The Blacks* in Berlin, Maya jumped at the opportunity. When she returned to Ghana several weeks later, Guy told his mother, "You have finished mothering a child. ... Now, I am a man. Your life is your own, and mine belongs to me." Not long before, Malcolm had written to Maya and asked her to work for the Organization for Afro-American Unity (OAAU), a group he had recently founded. Now that Guy was determined to be on his own, Maya realized she had no reason to stay in Ghana. She accepted the job. After four years abroad, Maya was returning home to the United States.

> "You have finished mothering a child. Now I am a man. Your life is your own, and mine belongs to me."
>
> – MAYA'S SON GUY

"I was an American. I realized that I was that more in Ghana [than] I ever realized in America," she said. "I realized that my mothers and fathers, and all their people, had enriched the soil of America with their sweat and tears and blood and flesh." ❖

Maya's first book, I Know Why the Caged Bird Sings, *turned her into a literary sensation. Her words brought to light the struggles of black people in the South.*

CHAPTER SEVEN

TURNING TRAGEDY INTO TRIUMPH

MAYA MADE SAN FRANCISCO HER FIRST STOP in the United States. When she got to town on Friday, February 19, 1965, she called Malcolm X. Maya told him she would be ready to start work after she visited her family. That weekend, Maya reconnected with her now-single mother and her beloved brother Bailey. Though Bailey was working in Hawaii at the time, he flew to California to welcome his little sister home.

On a bright Sunday morning on February 21, Maya went to visit her friend Lottie. The two were sharing memories in the dining room when the phone rang. It was another friend Ivonne calling to welcome Maya home. Ivonne asked Maya why she had returned to a country where people were crazy. "I mean, really crazy," she said. "Otherwise, why would they have just killed that man in New York?"

Maya (left) spent six months in Hawaii with Bailey (center). The time with her brother helped her come to terms with the murder of Malcolm X.

Maya pulled the phone from her ear and set it down on the table. She turned, walked into a bedroom, and locked the door. "I didn't have to ask," she later recalled. "I knew 'that man in New York' was Malcolm X and that someone had just killed him."

Maya was right. Malcolm X had been killed by members of the Nation of Islam. She was sad, stunned, and angry. As he had so often in life, Bailey came to rescue his sister. He convinced her to move to Hawaii and start singing again. Though she went with her brother and resumed a singing career, Maya's heart just wasn't in it. She turned her thoughts once again to writing. Maya was excited at the idea of putting pen to paper. She left Hawaii after six months, determined to pursue a career as a writer.

RISING FROM THE ASHES

Maya settled in Los Angeles and took a part-time job conducting door-to-door research about women's products. Her territory was in Watts. This struggling neighborhood had once been bright and thriving. Now, rampant unemployment and high prices were driving people in the community to frustration and anger. Families were stressed and schools were failing.

The growing tensions in Watts finally bubbled over on August 11, 1965. Rioters set fire to buildings and looted stores. Police, politicians, and the media descended on the chaos. They described the scene, but not the cause. Instead they blamed blacks for the destruction without asking why they were so angry.

The Watts Riots

On August 11, 1965, a white police officer stopped a black man on suspicion of driving drunk. As the officer and the man argued, the driver's mother entered the fray. She began yelling at the officer as a crowd of angry people gathered. The crowd grew hostile when the driver, his brother, and his mother were arrested. More police were called to the scene, but by that time the rioters had already started fires and begun looting buildings. The violence and destruction lasted nearly a week. When it was all over, 34 people were dead, more than 1,000 were injured, and nearly 4,000 had been arrested.

The Watts Riots in August 1965 brought attention to the economic and social disparities blacks faced. The riots also inspired Maya's writing.

During the second day of rioting, Maya went to the neighborhood to see the destruction for herself. "The smell had turned putrid as plastic furniture and supermarket meat departments smoldered," she remembers "Smoke and screams carried in the air. ... It became hard to discern if the figures brushing past me were male or female, young or old."

Maya wanted to tell the world what she saw. She planned to use her writings to express the voice of black America. She also decided to move back to the East Coast. She had barely begun packing when she received bad news. Guy, who had returned to San Francisco three days earlier, had been hit by a truck. He was in the hospital in serious condition. His neck was broken again.

Thankfully, Guy had cheated death once again. Maya stayed by her son's side for weeks. Only after Guy was well enough to sit up in bed at his grandmother's house did Maya feel she could leave for New York.

By the middle of 1967, Maya was with the Harlem Writers Guild in New York. She resumed her friendship with the writer James Baldwin and formed a new sister-friendship with Dolly McPherson. Thanks to the financial support of a friend, Maya was writing full time. By early 1968, she had completed two plays and was working on a group of poems.

TRAGEDY STRIKES AGAIN

On the evening of April 4, 1968, Maya was getting ready for a party. It was her 40th birthday, and she was planning a huge celebration. She looked around her apartment one last time to make sure everything was ready for her guests. Suddenly, the ringing of the telephone pulled Maya from her happy thoughts. It was her friend Dolly McPherson calling.

Maya could tell immediately that something was terribly wrong. Dolly made her promise not to turn on the radio or television or even answer the phone until she could get there. When her friend arrived, Maya found out that the news was worse than anything she could have imagined. Her friend Martin Luther King Jr. had been shot. He was dead.

Maya and King had kept in touch in the seven years since she'd worked for the Southern Christian Leadership Conference. Just weeks before his death, King had called Maya to ask for her help. He wanted her to help him organize the Poor People's

March on Washington, D.C. Maya agreed to work for King for one month. She was supposed to begin work on April 5, the day after her birthday.

In the days that followed King's assassination, depression wrapped itself around Maya. She later recalled:

The fact that he was a hero to me. The fact that he was of such importance to my country, to my people, to the time, all of those facts must take backstage to the truth that he was killed on my birthday. That my friend was killed on my birthday.

King's Call to Memphis

A sanitation workers' strike had drawn Martin Luther King Jr. to Memphis, Tennessee, in April 1968. The workers, who were nearly all black, wanted better pay and safer conditions. On April 3, King delivered his famous "Mountaintop" speech. He said, in part: "Like anybody, I would like to live a long life. Longevity has its place. But I'm not concerned about that now. I just want to do God's will. And He's allowed me to go up to the mountain. And I've looked over. And I've seen the Promised Land. I may not get there with you. But I want you to know tonight, that we, as a people, will get to the Promised Land!" Martin Luther King was killed the next day as he left his room at the Lorraine Motel.

Maya's friendship with Dolly McPherson (right) was a source of comfort and joy in good times and bad.

Maya could barely move, and her desire to speak fled. Her family and friends worried that she might stop speaking completely—just as she had when she was a little girl.

Concerned friends brought her food and checked in on her for weeks, but Maya remained inconsolable. It was her friend, the writer James Baldwin, who was finally able to pull her from her sadness.

Baldwin decided that what Maya needed was a laugh. A few weeks after King's death, he invited her to dinner with his friends cartoonist Jules Feiffer and his wife, Judy. The four spent the evening sharing funny stories about their childhoods. Maya got the group laughing with descriptions of her childhood in Stamps. Maya knew there was nothing funny about racism. She also realized that sometimes the oppressed have to find humor in their situation.

On the way home, Baldwin talked to Maya about the survival of African Americans. He told her:

We put surviving into our poems and into our songs. We put it into our folk tales. We danced surviving in Congo Square in New Orleans and put it in our pots when we cooked our pinto beans. We wore surviving on our backs when we clothed ourselves in the colors of the rainbow. We were pulled down so low we could hardly lift our eyes, so we knew, if we wanted to survive, we had better lift our own spirits. So we laughed whenever we got the chance.

Maya knew from experience that her friend was right.

James Baldwin

James Baldwin (1924–1987) first gained attention with his debut novel, *Go Tell It on the Mountain*. The book was based on his troubled childhood in Harlem. In 1963, just as the civil rights movement was exploding, Baldwin's book of essays *The Fire Next Time* was published. In the book, he called for all Americans to come to terms with the past and create a new future together. It was a best seller.

Maya and James Baldwin (left) shared a close connection. James encouraged Maya to write about her childhood for the book that became I Know Why the Caged Bird Sings.

LIFTING HER OWN SPIRITS

A few weeks later, Maya received a phone call from Robert Loomis. He was an editor at Random House publishers. Judy Feiffer had told Loomis about Maya's childhood stories. Now he was calling to ask if Maya would be interested in writing a book about her life.

Maya refused. She was a poet and playwright, she argued, not a novelist. Maya hung up and put the conversation out of her mind. She was busy preparing for a trip. In late spring 1968, Maya left for a two-month stay in California. Much to her surprise, Loomis called her again while she was away. Maya repeated that she was not interested in writing her autobiography.

The day before she was set to return home, Loomis gave it one more shot. He called Maya again to offer her the chance to write a book. This time though, he changed his approach. "You may be right not to attempt an autobiography," Loomis said. "It is nearly impossible to write autobiography as literature. Almost impossible."

Maya took the bait. She couldn't resist the challenge. "Well, maybe I will try it," she told Loomis. "I don't know how it will turn out, but I can try."

Maya decided to stay in California and got to work the next day. Sitting down at her mother's kitchen table, yellow notepad in hand, she thought about the human spirit. She wondered where people like Dr. King found the courage to remain standing in the face of misfortune. As she sat there thinking, she remembered the words of a poem from her childhood and wrote them down: "What you looking at me for? I didn't come to stay."

"[Maya Angelou] writes like a song, and like the truth. The wisdom, rue, and humor of her storytelling are borne on a lilting rhythm completely her own."

– ANNIE GOTTLIEB,
THE NEW YORK TIMES BOOK REVIEW

Years later, she recalled how she felt at that moment. Finally, that morning, she realized that, yes, she had come to stay. She had grown from a little girl who felt alone and rootless into a woman who had found her roots and learned to stand tall against adversity.

Maya's first autobiography, *I Know Why the Caged Bird Sings*, became a best seller when it was published in 1970. The title came from the poem "Sympathy," by Paul Laurence Dunbar. It was nominated for a National Book Award, one of the highest honors in literature, that same year.

Paul Laurence Dunbar

The title *I Know Why the Caged Bird Sings* was inspired by one of Maya's favorite Paul Laurence Dunbar poems, "Sympathy." Paul Dunbar (1872–1906) was the first African American poet to achieve national prominence. The son of former slaves, Dunbar wrote of the struggles of African Americans and their fight for equal rights. During his short life, he wrote 12 books of poetry, five novels, four books of short stories, and a play.

Annie Gottlieb wrote in *The New York Times* Book Review that Maya was a person who "writes like a song, and like the truth. The wisdom, rue, and humor of her storytelling are borne on a lilting rhythm completely her own."

Maya's groundbreaking book exposed a way of life in the Deep South that most people did not know existed. *I Know Why the Caged Bird Sings* remains one of the nation's most popular books and is required reading in schools across the country. But it is also banned in many schools because of the harsh experiences it recounts. Maya's autobiography describes in stark detail what it was like to be a young black girl growing up in the segregated South. In *I Know Why the Caged Bird Sings* Maya shares her most difficult life experiences—including rape, abandonment, and a fractured adolescence—as well as how she ultimately learned to survive, and thrive, on her own. ❖

Maya's life experiences proved to be ideal material for her poems, plays, and other writings.

CHAPTER EIGHT

THE WRITER EMERGES

WHEN *I KNOW WHY THE CAGED BIRD SINGS* was published in 1970, it earned brilliant reviews and legions of fans for Maya. Thanks to the book, she was recognized as one of America's best writers, but that was just the beginning.

When Maya was a little girl, she read the words of poems out loud to give them life. Her dream had always been to have her own poems published and read aloud. That dream came true in 1971 when her first collection of poems, *Just Give Me a Cool Drink of Water 'fore I Diiie,* was published. The 38 poems explored what it means to be a black woman in the United States.

Maya's writing was celebrated by many because it captured the voice of African Americans. Yet her words had meaning for people of other races, as well. They also lent themselves beautifully to being read aloud. "I write for the voice, not the eye,"

Maya has said. The first stanza of her poem "Harlem Hopscotch" is just one example of what the poet means:

One foot down, then hop! It's hot.
Good things for the ones that's got.
Another jump, now to the left.
Everybody for hisself.

Just Give Me a Cool Drink of Water 'fore I Diiie became a best seller and was nominated for a Pulitzer Prize in 1972. That same year, Maya became the first African American woman to have her own screenplay produced. *Georgia, Georgia* was the

In 1972, Maya traveled to Sweden to visit the set where her movie Georgia, Georgia *was being filmed.*

The Pulitzer Prize

Joseph Pulitzer (1847–1911) was a Hungarian-born, American journalist and newspaper owner. In his will, Pulitzer left instructions and the money to establish an award to encourage excellence in journalism. The first Pulitzer Prizes were awarded in 1917. Today, 21 awards are available every year. They are given for excellence in journalism, literature, poetry, photography, drama, and music. The Pulitzer Prize is considered one of the highest honors awarded in these fields.

story of a romance between a black singer and a white photographer. The movie was filmed in Sweden in 1972, and Maya went across the Atlantic Ocean to offer any help she could. Maya was disappointed that producers had hired a white man to direct the film. The experience strengthened her resolve to tell the African American story herself. She decided to learn how to direct.

Though Maya was busy writing, she managed to find time for a new relationship. In 1972, while she was traveling in England, Maya met and fell in love with Paul Du Feu. Du Feu spotted Maya at a party. Before the night was over, the Welshman came up to her to let her know she was the most beautiful woman in the world. After a brief courtship, Maya and Du Feu married in 1973 and moved to Sonoma, California. They were married for about eight years.

Alex Haley's book Roots *was turned into one of the most successful television series of all time. Maya had a part in her friend's miniseries. She played the grandmother of the story's protagonist.*

Maya moved back to New York for a short time in 1973 when she accepted a role in the Broadway play called *Look Away.* Though Maya preferred to focus on writing, she took the role because she wanted her costar to perform in a play she had written. The play closed soon after its debut, but Maya was nominated for a Tony Award for her performance. (The Tony Award is the highest honor a stage actor can achieve.)

Maya had conquered writing and acting. Now she set her sites on directing. She attended film school in Sweden in 1973. In early 1974, Maya returned to Los Angeles and enrolled at the American Film Institute.

During this time, Maya's second autobiography, *Gather Together in My Name,* was published. The book told the story of her early years as a struggling mother. In 1976, her third autobiography, *Singin' and Swingin' and Gettin' Merry Like Christmas*, was published. That book dealt with her first marriage and her beginning years as a performer.

In 1975, Maya's second book of poetry, *Oh Pray My Wings Are Gonna Fit Me Well*, was published. The poems in this book honor the struggles of her black ancestors. They call on the reader to appreciate and remember the history of African Americans.

In 1977, Maya was once again lured back into acting when she was asked to appear in her friend Alex Haley's miniseries *Roots*. The series, which was based on Haley's book, tells the story of seven generations—from their roots in Africa to America in the seventies. Maya accepted the role of Ngo Buto, the grandmother of the story's hero, Kunta Kinte. She also agreed to direct two installments of the miniseries. *Roots* was a huge success, and

Alex Haley's Roots

Roots: The Saga of an American Family tells the story of Alex Haley's Gambian ancestor, Kunta Kinte, who was sold into slavery, and the generations that followed him. The book earned Haley a Pulitzer Prize in 1977 and was made into a television miniseries that same year. The miniseries featured an all-star cast, including LeVar Burton, John Amos, Ben Vereen, Madge Sinclair, Leslie Uggams, and Louis Gossett Jr. It was one of the most watched television programs ever aired. Nearly 100 million viewers, or about half the country, watched the series.

Maya received an Emmy nomination for her moving portrayal of Ngo. (The Emmy Awards are the most prestigious honors for television performances.)

In 1978, *And Still I Rise,* another book of poems, was published. This collection contained one of Maya's most well-known poems "Still I Rise." The poem describes the will to survive—both of the poet and of all who have had to fight against adversity. One of its most recited passages includes the lines:

You may write me down in history
With your bitter, twisted lies,
You may trod me in the very dirt
But still, like dust, I'll rise.

Maya had taken the pain, struggle, and courage of the African American experience and, through her poems, plays, and films, shared those experiences with the world. Though her stories are about the black experience, they speak to people of all backgrounds. All she was doing, she has said, was writing about the world as she saw it. "My work is to be honest," she explained. "My work is to try to think clearly, then have the courage to make sure that what I say is the truth."

'A TEACHER WHO WRITES'

By the early 1980s, Maya had spent a great deal of her time putting words down onto her trademark yellow notepads. One thing she loved about writing was the ability to teach about life through her own wisdom and experiences. She got the opportunity to talk to her students face to face in 1981.

Wake Forest University in Winston-Salem, North Carolina, offered Maya the title Reynolds Professor of American Studies. She accepted. Despite the fact that she'd never graduated from college, Maya was about to become a college professor. Since 1981, she has been teaching on subjects ranging from history to ethics to poetry. The experience offered Maya the chance to discover something new about herself. "I'm not a writer who teaches," she said. "I'm a teacher who writes." Although her position requires that she teach one semester a year, the teacher always finds time to write.

Maya never does her writing at home, though. "[E]very room is filled with paintings, memories and every excuse to be lackadaisical or to be distracted," she explains. "Every excuse. And there goes my great idea." That's why, since moving to North Carolina in 1981, Maya has followed the same routine when she writes. Each morning at about 6 A.M. she checks into a local hotel room. Then, armed with a thermos of coffee, her yellow notepads, pens, a thesaurus, and a dictionary, she goes to work.

> **"My work is to be honest. My work is to try to think clearly, then have the courage to make sure that what I say is the truth."**
>
> – MAYA ANGELOU

In 1981, Maya's fourth autobiography, *The Heart of a Woman,* was published. The period covered in this book includes her journey to New York to join the Harlem Writers Guild and her civil rights work. It also details her relationships with Martin Luther King Jr. and Malcolm X. The book ends as Maya departs for Africa.

Maya wrote poems for Poetic Justice, *a film directed by Jon Singleton (right). She also had a small role in the movie.*

In 1986, she picked up the story in her fifth autobiography, *All God's Children Need Traveling Shoes,* which describes her time in Ghana. Maya also continued to write poetry, and as the years passed her works grew in popularity. By the end of the decade, she had published three more books of poems: *Shaker, Why Don't You Sing* in 1983, *Now Sheba Sings the Song* in 1987, and *I Shall Not Be Moved* in 1990.

In 1992, Maya was asked to write poems for the movie *Poetic Justice.* The film was about a young poet played by Janet Jackson. Maya also had a small part in the movie and befriended the film's other star, rapper Tupac Shakur. As her poetry reached a wider audience, Maya's words were becoming more and more a part of the American consciousness.

A VOICE FOR ALL AGES

Maya Angelou's words and teachings appeal to people of all ages. In addition to the books and poems that are typically aimed at an older audience, she has written the children's book *Mrs. Flowers*. The story tells of her relationship with the woman from her youth who introduced her to the power of the spoken word and helped her find her own voice. She also published a book of poems for children called *Life Doesn't Frighten Me*. Kids and adults have even caught the author on *Sesame Street* where she's played hand-clapping games with Elmo and helped Baby Natasha learn the letter N. ❖

Maya's joy of life led her to explore many creative outlets. In 1997, she treated fans to a rare performance at the Essence Music Festival.

CHAPTER NINE

A GLORIOUS LEGACY

IN 2002, MAYA'S SIXTH AUTOBIOGRAPHY, *A SONG Flung Up to Heaven,* was published. It was not an easy book to write. In fact, *A Song Flung Up to Heaven* was so difficult for Maya to work on that she decided she would not write another autobiography. As the writer explained:

> *The book had to deal with situations that didn't seem to have any hope in them—the murder of Malcolm X, the murder of Martin Luther King on my birthday and the uprising in Watts. I thought everything I write says that you may encounter many defeats, but you must not be defeated. I couldn't see how I could find hope writing all these negatives. So I've written that book for six years, and it's the slimmest of all my books.*

SOMETHING FOR EVERYONE

Maya might have given up on writing autobiographies, but she would never give up writing completely. She even expanded into a whole new medium: greeting cards.

In 2002, Maya began working with Hallmark on what would become the "Maya Angelou Life in Celebration" collection—greeting cards that feature her writings. When it was announced that the accomplished author and poet would be working with a greeting card company, Maya received some criticism. Some people said that writing greeting cards was beneath her. Perhaps that's what Maya was thinking at first, too. She turned down the

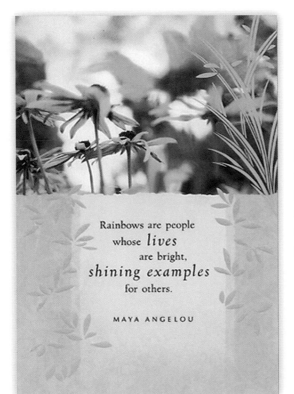

Rainbows are people
whose *lives*
are bright,
shining examples
for others.

MAYA ANGELOU

It is important to Maya that she spread her messages of hope and courage. She saw writing for Hallmark as one more way to make her voice heard.

company's offer many times before finally agreeing to the idea. After meeting with people from Hallmark and thinking more about the opportunity, Maya realized that working with the card company was exactly the right fit for her. "If I'm America's poet, or one of them, then I want to be in people's hands," the author later explained. "All people's hands, people who would never buy a book."

The process of writing for Hallmark was exciting for Maya. "What I can take two pages writing about, I have to say in two sentences," she says. "It's delicious. It helps me to get my language and have control of it. It's poetic musings, it's poetic thinking ... it's what it feels like to be a human being."

> **"If I'm America's poet, or one of them, then I want to be in people's hands. All people's hands, people who would never buy a book."**
>
> – MAYA ANGELOU

In 2004, Maya tried her hand at yet another style of writing. She wrote *Hallelujah! The Welcome Table: A Lifetime of Memories with Recipes*. The cookbook features some of Maya's favorite recipes and related family memories.

Maya's respect for and recognition of her family and her history are central to her life and her writing. In 2007, she had the chance to honor her African ancestors when she was asked to speak at the dedication ceremony for the African Burial Ground National Monument in New York City. The site honors the thousands of people who died on America's shores after being taken from their homelands and forced into slavery.

African Burial Ground

In 1991, construction workers in lower Manhattan discovered what turned out to be the largest known intact colonial African cemetery in the United States. The remains of more than 400 slaves were uncovered, but historians and archaeologists say that up to 20,000 men, women, and children of African descent were buried in the 6.6-acre (2.7-hectare) site in the 17th and 18th centuries. In 2006, the site was declared a national monument. National monuments are areas of land set aside for protection from development that aim to preserve a unique resource.

Maya read a poem during the dedication ceremony for the African Burial Ground National Monument in New York on October 5, 2007.

Maya spoke for her ancestors when she said: "You may bury me in the bottom of Manhattan. I will rise. My people will get me. I will rise out of the huts of history's shame."

Today, Maya lives in Winston-Salem, North Carolina, and Harlem, New York. Sharing her time with friends and family is of the utmost importance to her. Her brother and mother are gone now, but Maya believes they are with her always.

Maya's son Guy is also a writer. When asked if he felt he grew up in his mother's shadow, Guy replies, "No, I didn't. I grew up in her light." Guy has a son, Colin, who has made his Grandma Maya a great-grandmother, too! Maya also considers her closest friends to be part of her family.

MAYA'S SISTER-FRIEND

One person Maya counts among her closest friends is talk-show host Oprah Winfrey. The two women met in the late 1970s when Oprah was just starting out as a news anchor. Winfrey begged the author for a five-minute interview—and impressed her when she didn't take a second more than what she had requested. The two have been "sister-mother-daughter" friends ever since.

Oprah said she felt connected to Maya from the first time she read *I Know Why the Caged Bird Sings*. According to Oprah:

> It was the first book I ever read that made me feel my life as a colored girl growing up in Mississippi deserved validation. Meeting Maya on those pages was like meeting myself in full. For the first time, as a young black girl, my experience was validated.

Maya's book of essays *Wouldn't Take Nothing for My Journey Now* was dedicated to Oprah, and another book *Even the Stars Look Lonesome* contains an essay praising her friend. Oprah regularly has Maya as a guest on her television show. "Today Maya is a kind of quintessential Everywoman: essayist, entertainer, activist, poet, professor, film director, and mother ..." Oprah has said. "She's the woman who can share my triumphs, chide me with hard truth and soothe me with words of comfort when I call her in my deepest pain."

In 2006, Oprah asked Maya to host a weekly program on Oprah & Friends Radio. Each week, listeners are treated to Maya's insights on issues such as race, age, and religion.

Among Maya's most cherished relationships is her "sister-mother-daughter" friendship with Oprah Winfrey.

A VOICE FOR THE WORLD

Maya Angelou's understanding of the human experience and her ability to translate the fears, joys, and hopes of people of all creeds has made hers the voice that people choose to represent them again and again. Fittingly, Maya was asked to write and read a poem for the 50th anniversary of the founding of the United Nations on June 26, 1995.

The last stanzas of the poem, "A Brave and Startling Truth," convey the lifetime of wisdom of this great American voice. In Maya's words we see the courage and compassion that have been gained through decades of love, loss, tragedy, and triumph:

When we come to it
We, this people, on this wayward, floating body
Created on this earth, of this earth
Have the power to fashion for this earth
A climate where every man and every woman
Can live freely without sanctimonious piety
Without crippling fear

When we come to it
We must confess that we are the possible
We are the miraculous, the true wonder of this world
That is when, and only when
We come to it. ❖

TIME LINE

1928 Maya Angelou is born Marguerite Johnson on April 4 in St. Louis, Missouri.

1931 Marguerite and her brother, Bailey, are sent on a train to live with their grandmother in Stamps, Arkansas.

1935 Marguerite moves to St. Louis, Missouri, to live with her mother. After being sexually abused by her mother's boyfriend, Marguerite returns to Stamps.

1941 Marguerite moves to San Francisco, California, to live with her mother.

1944 Marguerite is hired as the first black streetcar driver in San Francisco, California.

1945 Marguerite graduates from high school; her son Guy is born.

1951 Marguerite meets and marries Tosh Angelos.

1953 Marguerite gets divorced, changes her name to Maya Angelou, and takes a job as a Calypso singer at a club called The Purple Onion.

1954-1955 Maya tours Europe, Israel, and Egypt with the stage production of *Porgy and Bess*.

1956 Maya returns to California to care for her son.

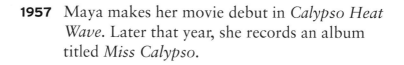

1957 Maya makes her movie debut in *Calypso Heat Wave*. Later that year, she records an album titled *Miss Calypso*.

1959 Maya moves to Brooklyn, New York, with her son Guy and joins the Harlem Writers Guild.

1960 Maya begins working for Martin Luther King Jr. as the northern coordinator of the Southern Christian Leadership Conference (SCLC). In the fall she meets and falls in love with South African freedom fighter Vus Make.

1961-1965 Maya lives in Egypt and Ghana where she works as an editor and a newspaper columnist.

1965 Maya's friend Malcolm X is assassinated in New York City on February 21. The Watts Riots rage in Los Angeles from August 11 to August 15.

1968 Martin Luther King Jr. is assassinated in Memphis, Tennessee, on April 4—Maya's 40th birthday. Maya writes and produces the 10-part series *Blacks, Blues, Black* for PBS.

1970 Maya's first autobiography, *I Know Why the Caged Bird Sings*, is published. It's later nominated for a National Book Award.

1971 Maya's book of poetry *Just Give Me a Cool Drink of Water 'Fore I Diiie* is nominated for a Pulitzer Prize; she marries Paul Du Feu.

1974 Maya's second autobiography, *Gather Together in My Name,* is published.

1976 *Singin' and Swingin' and Gettin' Merry Like Christmas,* Maya's third autobiography, is published.

1977 Maya appears in the TV miniseries *Roots.*

1981 Maya's fourth autobiography, *The Heart of a Woman,* is published. She accepts a lifetime appointment as Reynolds Professor of American Studies at Wake Forest University in Winston-Salem, North Carolina.

1986 *All God's Children Need Traveling Shoes,* Maya's fifth autobiography, is published.

1993 Maya reads her poem "On the Pulse of Morning" at President Clinton's first inauguration on January 21.

1995 Maya delivers her poem "A Brave and Startling Truth" at a celebration of the 50th anniversary of the United Nations on June 26.

2002 Maya's sixth and final autobiography, *A Song Flung Up to Heaven,* is published.

2008 Maya celebrates her 80th birthday on April 4; her friends and family write the book *A Glorious Celebration* in her honor. Maya publishes the book *Letter to My Daughter.*

A CONVERSATION WITH
Wanda Phipps

Wanda Phipps is the author of several books of poetry, including Field of Wanting *and* Wake-Up Calls: 66 Morning Poems. *She was featured on MTV's* Spoken Word II *and is a founder of Yara Arts Group, a theater company. Here, Wanda talks about Maya Angleou's work and legacy.*

Q. How has Maya's work influenced or inspired you?

A. I remember reading Maya Angelou's autobiographies and being inspired by the story of her life and how she was able to use her difficult experiences to create poetry. I am always amazed and inspired by the power of creativity to transform suffering into art.

Q. Why do you think it is important for people to read and hear poetry?

A. I think it is important for people to not only hear and read poetry, but to write it as well. It is a way of knowing and looking at the world and yourself that helps you to see things differently. It has the power to shift your perspective. Poetry can allow you to … peek into the lives and cultures of others. Poetry can capture a complex moment of revelation or inspiration and communicate that to a reader or simply describe in vivid detail the suffering, joy, and beauty found by someone a million miles away from you. There is a kind of magic there.

Q. Do you have a favorite Angelou poem?

A. I remember particularly loving her famous poem "Phenomenal Woman." I was really struck by the way the poem celebrates the strength, beauty, and power of women and female energy. I saw bits of it performed once on television as part of a stage production of her work. I love … when poetry comes alive in performance.

Q. Maya Angelou's poems are appreciated by people all over the world. What is it about her poetry that makes it possible to reach so many different people?

A. The universality of human experience is communicated in poetry. Anyone can identify with and understand basic human emotions like joy, pain, sorrow, love, and grief—and poetry investigates those territories clothed in the details of everyday life. Poetry can explore the simple beauty of words: rhythm, sound, movement, rhyme, and more. All of these things can be felt and heard even if you don't know a particular language. Poetry has a unique capacity to speak to the heart as well as the mind, body, and spirit.

Q. Maya Angelou turned to writing as a way to cope with a difficult childhood. When did you realize you wanted to be a writer? Did writing help you deal with the challenges you experienced growing up?

A. I don't think I ever realized I wanted to be a writer. I just started doing it in the third grade and never stopped. I initially fell in love with rhythm and rhymes and the magical nature of words. I fell in love with their ability to be like little incantations, little spells to conjure up joy. And when I shared [my poems] with [other people], I fell in love with the pleasure it brought them.

I think writing poetry helped me through difficult times as a child and still helps me now. It helps in any difficult situation simply to express what you feel in words. There is also the pleasure of writing itself [and] the pleasure of enjoying the finished piece—turning pain into art. You've taken something horrible and from that raw life material at least attempted to create something [beautiful].

Q. What do you think young people today can learn from Maya Angelou?

A. Maya Angelou's work will continue to influence future generations. Young people today can learn from her example, from her courage, her strength, pride and humility, her creativity, and the inspirational energy of her presence on this Earth. They can learn from her example to be true to themselves, to have the courage to live out their dreams, to persevere no matter what, and how to live a rich, joyous, and fruitful life.

GLOSSARY

activist: an especially active advocate for, or opponent against, a cause

adversity: a state of hardship or misfortune; a difficult time

ancestors: the people from whom one is descended

apartheid: a policy of racial segregation or discrimination

boarder: someone who pays a sum of money in return for regular meals and lodging

boycott: to abstain from buying or using something, generally in protest

catapulted: to have been suddenly thrown or thrust into a particular situation

civil rights: rights of citizens to political and social freedom and equality

colonialism: when a country rules or controls another nation, territory, or people

expatriate: someone who lives in a country other than his or her native country

impromptu: done without previous preparation

inadequacy: the state or condition of lacking in certain qualities; insufficiency

inauguration: the act or ceremony of officially beginning or being formally introduced

inconsolable: unable to be comforted

loot: to steal valuable goods

lynch: to execute without a legal trial, especially to hang, as by a mob

malign: to make harmful and untrue statements about someone

pacify: to bring or restore a state of peace

progeny: a descendant or an offspring

protagonist: the principal character in a literary work, such as a novel, play, or movie

racism: a hatred or an intolerance of people of another race or races

riot: disturbance of the peace by a crowd

rue: to feel sorrow or regret

satire: use of irony, sarcasm, or ridicule to expose the folly or vice of an individual or humankind

scourged: to have severely punished or criticized

segregation: enforced separation of racial or other groups

sit-in: sitting in the seats or on the floor of an establishment as a means of protest

speakeasy: a place where alcoholic beverages were illegally sold during the Prohibition era (1920–1933)

FOR MORE INFORMATION

BOOKS AND OTHER RESOURCES

Angelou, Maya. *All God's Children Need Traveling Shoes*. New York: Random House, Inc., 1986.

Angelou, Maya. *Gather Together in My Name*. New York: Random House, Inc., 1974.

Angelou, Maya. *The Heart of a Woman*. New York: Random House, Inc., 1981.

Angelou, Maya. *I Know Why the Caged Bird Sings*. New York: Random House, Inc., 1970.

Angelou, Maya. *Singin' and Swingin' and Gettin' Merry Like Christmas*. New York: Random House, Inc., 1976.

Angelou, Maya. *A Song Flung Up to Heaven*. New York: Random House, Inc., 2002.

Gillespie, Marcia, Rosa Johnson Butler and Richard A. Long. *Maya Angelou: A Glorious Celebration*.
New York: Doubleday, 2008.

WEB SITES

Academy of Achievement
www.achievement.org
Look up Maya Angelou on the American Academy of Achievement web site.

Maya Angelou
www.mayaangelou.com
Maya Angelou's official web site includes biographical information, recent interviews, and more.

SELECT BIBLIOGRAPHY AND SOURCE NOTES

Angelou, Maya. *All God's Children Need Traveling Shoes*. N.Y.: Random House, Inc., 1986.

Angelou, Maya. *I Know Why the Caged Bird Sings*. N.Y.: Random House, Inc., 1970.

Angelou, Maya. *A Song Flung Up to Heaven*. N.Y.: Random House, Inc., 2002.

Angelou, Maya. *Wouldn't Take Nothin' for My Journey Now*. N.Y.: Bantam Books, 1993.

PAGE 2
"Still I Rise," copyright © 1978 by Maya Angelou, from AND STILL I RISE by Maya Angelou. Used by Permission of Random House Inc.

CHAPTER ONE
Page 7, line 10: Gillespie, et al. *Maya Angelou: A Glorious Celebration*. N.Y.: Doubleday, 2008, p. 137

Page 9, line 12: Manegold, Catherine S. "An Afternoon with Maya Angelou: A Wordsmith at her Inaugural Anvil, *New York Times*, January 20, 1993

Page 9, line 25: "Blacks play biggest role in Clinton inauguration," *Jet*, February 8, 1993

Page 11, line 3: From ON THE PULSE OF MORNING by Maya Angelou, copyright © 1993 by Maya Angelou. Used by permission of Random House, Inc.

CHAPTER TWO
Page 14, line 12: Moore, Lucinda. "A Conversation with Maya Angelou at 75," *Smithsonian*, May 2008

Page 16, line 5: From I KNOW WHY THE CAGED BIRD SINGS by Maya Angelou, copyright © 1969 and renewed 1997 by Maya Angelou. Used by permission of Random House, Inc., p. 18

Page 17, line 8. Ibid.

Page 17, line 14: Ibid., p. 26

Page 19, line 4: Ibid, p. 52

Page 19, line 13: Ibid.

Page 19, line 23: Ibid., p. 23

Page 20, line 9: Ibid., p. 60

Page 20, line 24: Ibid., p. 65

Page 21, line 3: Ibid., p. 63

CHAPTER THREE
Page 25, line 4: From I KNOW WHY THE CAGED BIRD SINGS, p. 92

Page 26, line 12: Ibid., p. 93

Page 26, line 23: Ibid., p. 98

Page 27, line 4: Ibid., p. 100

Page 29, line 5: Ibid., p. 179

Page 29, line 12: Ibid., p. 180

Page 29, line 26: Ibid., p. 184

Page 30, sidebar: www.black-network.com/anthem.htm

Page 32, line 2: From I KNOW WHY THE CAGED BIRD SINGS, p. 189

Page 34, line 2: Ibid., p. 243

Page 34, line 10: Ibid.

Page 35, line 22: Ibid., p. 243

Page 35, line 26: Ibid., p. 245

Page 36, line 2: Ibid.

Page 37, line 6: Ibid., p. 254

CHAPTER FOUR
Page 40, line 4: From WOULDN'T TAKE NOTHING FOR MY JOURNEY NOW by Maya Angelou, copyright © 1993 by Maya Angelou. Used by permission of Random House, Inc., p. 28

Page 44, line 11: From SINGIN' AND SWINGIN' AND GETTIN' MERRY LIKE CHRISTMAS by Maya Angelou, copyright © 1969 and renewed 1997 by Maya Angelou. Used by permission of Random House, Inc., p. 129

Page 45, line 6: Ibid., p. 232

Page 45, line 8: Ibid.

Page 46, line 20: From THE HEART OF A WOMAN by Maya Angelou, copyright © 1981 by Maya Angelou. Used by permission of Random House, Inc., p. 8

CHAPTER FIVE

Page 49, line 6: From THE HEART OF A WOMAN, p. 38
Page 49, line 13: Ibid., p. 39
Page 51, line 14: Ibid., p. 56
Page 52, line 8: Ibid., p. 92
Page 53, line 10: Ibid., p. 95
Page 56, line 4: Ibid., p. 144
Page 56, line 14: Ibid., p. 145
Page 57, line 3: Ibid.
Page 57, line 23: Ibid., p. 167
Page 57, line 28: Ibid., p. 168
Page 59, line 1: Ibid.

CHAPTER SIX

Page 63, line 2: From ALL GOD'S CHILDREN NEED TRAVELING SHOES by Maya Angelou, copyright © 1986 by Maya Angelou. Used by permission of Random House, Inc., p. 1
Page 64, line 11: Frost, David. "An Interview with Maya Angelou," *The New Sun*
Page 64, line 17: "Angelou's fight–with poetry," News.bbc.co.uk, September 20, 2003
Page 67, line 13: From ALL GOD'S CHILDREN NEED TRAVELING SHOES, p. 185
Page 67, line 25: "Angelou's fight–with poetry"

CHAPTER SEVEN

Page 69, line 13: From A SONG FLUNG UP TO HEAVEN by Maya Angelou, copyright © 2002 by Maya Angelou. Used by permission of Random House, Inc., p. 24
Page 70, line 2: Ibid.
Page 72, line 2: Ibid., p. 67
Page 74, line 6: http://www.history.com/media.do?mediaType=All&searchTerm=maya+angelou&action=search&x=0&y=0&showName=-1, November 28, 1990
Page 74, sidebar: http://www.americanrhetoric.com/speeches/mlkivebeentothemountaintop.htm
Page 76, line 7: From A SONG FLUNG UP TO HEAVEN, p. 196

Page 78, lines 1–7: Ibid., p. 206
Page 78, line 14: From I KNOW WHY THE CAGED BIRD SINGS, p. 1
Page 79, line 2: Gottlieb, Annie. *New York Times Book Review,* June 16, 1974, accessed at poetryfoundation.org

CHAPTER EIGHT

Page 81, line 15: "America's Renaissance Woman," http://achievement.org
Page 82, line 3: "Harlem Hopscotch," copyright © 1971 by Maya Angelou from JUST GIVE ME A COOL DRINK OF WATER 'FORE I DIIIE by Maya Angelou. Used by permission of Random House, Inc.
Page 86, line 9: "Still I Rise," copyright © 1978 by Maya Angelou, from AND STILL I RISE by Maya Angelou. Used by permission of Random House, Inc.
Page 86, line 18: Smiley, Tavis. pbs.org
Page 87, line 7: "Maya Angelou celebrates her 80 years of pain and joy," *USA Today,* March 26, 2008
Page 87, line 12: Manegold. "An Afternoon with Maya Angelou"

CHAPTER NINE

Page 91, line 6: www.Oprah.com.
Page 93, line 4: Williams, Jeannie. "Maya Angelou pens her sentiment for Hallmark," *USA Today,* January 10, 2002
Page 93, line 12: Ibid.
Page 95, line 1: www.Africanburialground.gov
Page 95, line 9: www.Oprah.com, March 29, 2008
Page 95, line 19: Minzesheimer
Page 95, line 22: Cooper, Ilene. *Up Close: Oprah Winfrey.* N.Y.: Puffin Books, 2007, pp. 58–59
Page 96, line 4: Winfrey, Oprah. "Oprah's Cut with Maya Angelou," http://www2.oprah.com/omagazine/200012/omag_200012_maya_b.jhtml
Page 97, line 12: From A BRAVE AND STARTLING TRUTH by Maya Angelou, copyright © 1995 by Maya Angelou. Used by permission of Random House, Inc.

INDEX

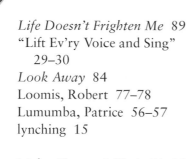

ABOUT THE AUTHOR

Jill Egan is a freelance writer who has written numerous stories about current events and the people who shape our world. When she's not writing, Jill enjoys exploring new places—both in person and through the pages of books. Jill is a native of Juneau, Alaska. She currently lives with her husband in San Francisco, California.

PICTURE CREDITS

Cover: © Marc Royce/Corbis; p. 2: Rick Mackler/Globe Photos; p. 6, 10, 100: Mark Lennihan/Associated Press; p. 12, 14, 16, 22, 24, 37, 41, 45, 55, 56, 63, 70, 75, 77, 85, 98: Courtesy of the Angelou-Johnson Archives; p. 18: Library of Congress; p. 21: MPI/Hulton Archive/Getty Images; p. 28, 50, 66, 72: Associated Press; p. 31: John Vacha/FPG/Getty Images; p. 34: Hans Wild/Time & Life Pictures/Getty Images; p. 38, 60: Michael Ochs Archives/Getty Images; p. 47: Gene Lester/Getty Images; p. 48: Edward A. Hausner/New York Times, Co./Getty Images; p. 52: Howard Sochurek/Time & Life Pictures/Getty Images; p. 58: Burt Shavitz/Pix Inc/Time & Life Pictures/Getty Images; p. 68: AP Photo/stf; p. 80: G. Marshall Wilson/Ebony Collection via AP Images; p. 82: Photofest; p. 88: Fotos International/Getty Images; p. 90: © Marc Brasz/Corbis; p. 92: Courtesy of Hallmark; p. 94: Bebeto Matthews/Associated Press; p. 96: Rose Hartman/Globe Photos, p. 101: Courtesy of Wanda Phipps, www.mindhoney.com.